Helping Children See Jesus

ISBN: 978-1-64104-040-2

THE SAVIOUR
Everybody Needs Jesus
New Testament Volume 3: Life of Christ Part 3

Author: Ruth B. Greiner
Illustrator: Frances H. Hertzler   Cover Art: Cassandre Maxwell
Computer Graphic Artist: Joshua Day
Typesetting and Layout: Patricia Pope

© 2018 Bible Visuals International
PO Box 153, Akron, PA 17501-0153
Phone: (717) 859-1131
www.biblevisuals.org

All rights reserved. No part of this publication may be reproduced, stored in a retrieval system or transmitted in any form by any means, electronic, mechanical, photocopy, recording or otherwise, without the prior permission of the publisher, except as provided by USA copyright law.

RELATED ITEMS

To access related items (such as activities, memory verse posters and translated texts) please visit our web store at shop.biblevisuals.org and enter 1003 in the search box on the page.

FREE TEXT DOWNLOAD

To access a FREE printable copy of the teaching text (PDF format) in English or other available languages, enter S1003DL in the search box. Add the item to your cart, and use coupon code XTACSV17 at checkout. Once your order is processed you will receive an email with a link to the free download.

The Father sent The Son to be The Saviour of the world.

1 John 4:14b

© Bible Visuals International Inc

Lesson 1
JESUS CALLS HIS DISCIPLES

Scripture to be studied: Matthew 3:1-17; Mark 1:1-11; Luke 3:1-18; John 1:15-51

The *aim* of the lesson: (1) The Lamb of God is the One who saves from sin. (2) He, the Sinless One, invites those who receive Him as sin-bearer, to follow Him in service.

What your students should *know*: Jesus wants them to come to Him and be His disciples.

What your students should *feel*: A desire to follow Jesus.

What your students should *do*:

Unsaved: Believe that Jesus, the Lamb of God, died for their sins and receive Him as Saviour.

Saved: Tell others that the Lord Jesus is the Lamb of God, the Saviour of the world.

Lesson outline (for the teacher's and students' notebooks):

1. Jesus Christ–the perfect sacrifice (Hebrews 10:4-14).
2. Following the Lamb of God (John 1:15-39).
3. Bringing others to Jesus (John 1:40-44).
4. Recognizing the Son of God (John 1:45-51).

The verse to be memorized:

The Father sent the Son to be the Saviour of the world. (1 John 4:14)

NOTE TO THE TEACHER

In all of your ministry, you should be careful and prayerful. This is especially important when teaching this volume. Because each lesson points to the Saviour, Satan will try to make the truths ineffective. But "greater is He that is in you, than he that is in the world" (1 John 4:4). Satan has power. The Son of God has *all* power.

In this first lesson you will be presenting the Lord Jesus as the Lamb of God. This will need careful explanation. Your students may know nothing about lambs being used as sacrifices. Take sufficient time at the beginning of the lesson to help them to understand the full meaning of John's referring to the Lord Jesus as "the Lamb of God."

Examine your own heart, teacher. Are *you* obediently following the Lord Jesus? Can you say (as did the Apostle Paul), "Be ye followers of me, even as I also am of Christ" (1 Corinthians 11:1)? You teach more by your life, than by your lips!

INTRODUCTION

Earlier in this series we learned of the coming of the Son of God to earth. We have studied about His birth, His death, His resurrection, and His ascension. Is this all there is to know about Him? No, indeed! There is much, much more. Starting with these lessons and continuing through several more volumes, we are going to learn about some of the things that happened between the birth and death of the Lord Jesus.

We know little of His childhood, except that once, when He was 12 years old, He was in the house of God with the religious leaders. (See Luke 2:42, 46.) They listened to Him, asked Him questions, and were "astonished at His understanding and answers" (Luke 2:47). After that we know nothing of Him until He was a grown man, about 30 years old. (See Luke 3:23.) Then for three years the Lord Jesus did so many things that, if they were all "written every one, I suppose that even the world itself could not contain the books that should be written." (See John 21:25.)

THE LESSON

1. JESUS CHRIST– THE PERFECT SACRIFICE
Hebrews 10:4-14

From the earliest times, we read in the Word of God about lambs. They were used as sacrifices. That is, when a person sinned he had to kill and burn his very best lamb. The lamb was the substitute that took the death punishment which the sinner deserved. (*Teacher:* See Genesis 4:4; 22:7; Exodus 12:3-6; 29:38-42; Numbers 28:9-19, 26, 27; 29:1, 2, 7, 8, 13-36; Leviticus 12:6; 14:10-18.)

Show Illustration #1

Before a man worshiped God, he offered a sacrifice for his sins. Uncounted numbers of lambs (and other animals) died in place of the sinner. Not one of these, however, could take away sin. One of the purposes of those sacrifices was to help the offerer to remember that some day there would come One sacrifice that would be absolutely perfect. He would be offered once. And that offering would be good for all people of all time. That One perfect sacrifice is the Lord Jesus Christ. (See Hebrews 10:4-14.)

Before the Son of God came to earth, many wrote that He would come. One said of Him: "He is brought as a lamb to the slaughter" (Isaiah 53:7). That was written more than 700 years before the Lord Jesus was born! It was meant to help people understand that the Son of God would suffer death.

That same prophet (Isaiah) told also that when the Son of God would come to earth, His coming would be announced by one who would cry out the news in the wilderness. (See Isaiah 40:3-5.)

Finally, exactly as the prophet had written so many hundreds of years before, a man did preach in the wilderness. His name was John the Baptist. He went up and down the Jordan River telling about Someone special who would come. Because it was wild country, John wore rough clothing made of camel hair. He ate what he found as he traveled: locusts and wild honey. Crowds of people came from the cities to hear John the Baptist preach. He explained that they had to repent of [turn from] their sins and be baptized in the Jordan River to show that they were truly sorry for their sins. Many people did repent and were baptized.

Always he spoke of the One who soon would come–One, he explained, who was far greater than he, John the Baptist. "I am not even worthy to unfasten His shoes," he said.

2. FOLLOWING THE LAMB OF GOD
John 1:15-39

Show Illustration #2

One day when John the Baptist and two of his disciples [followers], were together in the wilderness, he saw a Man nearby and said, "Look! There is the Lamb of God!"

The Lamb of God! That moment those two men knew that the One of whom Isaiah the prophet had written and about whom John the Baptist had preached, had come. And immediately both men turned from following the preacher in the wilderness to follow the Lamb of God.

When He saw them following Him, He asked, "What do you want?"

They answered, "Where do you live?"

"Come and see," He said.

The two men, whose names were Andrew and John, went to the place where the Lamb of God had been staying. But they were not really interested in the place where He lived. They wanted to be with Him. They wanted to know more about Him, "the Lamb of God." They did not want to leave Him.

Who was the Lamb of God? He was the Lord Jesus Christ, the One who had come to be the Saviour of the world. He was the One for whom Andrew and John and others had been waiting. Hundreds of years before, God had promised that He would come. Now these two were seeing Him with their very own eyes! And they were with Him.

What He told them that day, we do not know. But this we know: from that time on they were never the same. Never again would they live as they had lived before. Instead, leaving their homes and families, they followed the Lamb of God.

3. BRINGING OTHERS TO JESUS
John 1:40-44

Show Illustration #3

Later that same day, Andrew hurried to his brother, Simon. "We have found the Messiah, the One sent by God!" Andrew exclaimed. And immediately he brought his brother Simon to the Son of God.

The moment the Lord Jesus saw Simon, He said, "You are Simon, the son of John. But you shall be called Peter, a stone." Imagine that! The Son of God knew the name of the man; He knew whose son he was. And He changed the name of Simon. It was as if the Lord Jesus had said, "You are going to be a rock-like man. You are going to stand firmly for the truth. Your name is a stone." (There was no way that Simon Peter could know right then all that the Lord Jesus meant.)

Andrew and John and Simon Peter were delighted. They had found the Messiah, the Lamb of God. More than that, they were now His disciples. The next day when Jesus saw Philip, He called, "Come with Me." And Philip promptly and obediently followed the Lamb of God. Now there were four disciples: Andrew and John, Simon Peter and Philip.

4. RECOGNIZING THE SON OF GOD
John 1:45-51

Show Illustration #4

Philip could not keep the good news to himself. He hurried to his friend, Nathanael. "Nathanael," he said, "we have found the Messiah. He is the very One about whom Moses and the prophets spoke. He is Jesus of Nazareth."

"Nazareth!" Nathanael exclaimed. "Can any good thing come out of Nazareth?" Nazareth was such a small, unimportant town that it seemed to Nathanael quite impossible for the Saviour of the world to come from there.

Philip did not argue with Nathanael. He simply said, "Come and see for yourself."

When they hurried to Jesus, Jesus said of Nathanael, "Here comes an honest man–a true son of Israel."

Nathanael was surprised, asking, "How do you know me?"

"I could see you under the fig tree before Philip found you," Jesus explained.

The Lord Jesus had seen Nathanael before Philip had called him. The Lord knew who Nathanael was. For He knows everything!

Nathanael exclaimed, "You are the Son of God."

Yes, the Son of God had come. And now Nathanael joined the other four who followed Him.

Later the Lord Jesus chose seven more men, making a total of 12 disciples. For the next three years those men were to be learners of the things of God. The Son of God Himself would be their teacher. They were to see amazing miracles. (We will learn of the first one in our next lesson.) They would follow Him in and out of towns and cities. They were to see and hear Him talk to one person and another about the only way of having life eternal. Though they did not understand it, they were to hear from His own lips that He, the Lamb of God, would suffer and die and rise again the third day. (See Mark 9:31, 32; 10:33, 34; Luke 18:31-34; Matthew 20:17-19.) Then after the Lord Jesus would ascend to God the Father, the disciples were to teach others the things that they had learned from Him. So the disciples left everything they had to follow the Saviour, the Lamb of God.

We, too, can be followers of the Son of God. First, however, we must believe that He is the Son of God. We must believe that He, the Lamb of God, died for our sins. We must receive Him as our own personal Saviour.

Once you belong to Him, you are known as His disciple, His pupil, His follower. He wants you to be like Andrew and Philip– eager to tell others the wonderful news that the Lord Jesus is the Lamb of God, the Saviour of the world.

Lesson 2
JESUS FIRST MIRACLE

NOTE TO THE TEACHER

The first miracle that the Lord Jesus did is recorded in only one place: John 2:1-11. Before reading further, study carefully that portion of Scripture. Then make a study (in other parts of the Bible) of truths that appear in this little section.

1. For example, study Scriptures which deal with the subject of wine. (See Genesis 14:18; 27: 28; Leviticus 23:13; Judges 9:13; Luke 10:34; 1 Timothy 5:23.) Someone may question why the Lord Jesus turned water into an intoxicating drink. The answer is that we do not believe He made anything intoxicating. What He doubtless provided was the sweet, pure juice of grapes. He *could* have made a fermented drink if He had chosen to. But He never did anything that was harmful. The Word of God gives much space to the danger of drinking intoxicating wine. (For example, see Proverbs 20:1; 23:29, 32; Ephesians 5:18.) Our Lord never did anything contrary to God's Word.

   In many lands, even today, the water is unsafe for drinking. This may have been true in Cana. Thus it was necessary to have a substitute. That the Lord Jesus could take even impure water and make it into a safe, delicious drink–that He could do it in a moment–is indeed a miracle!

2. Why was it necessary for the Lord Jesus to do miracles? He had come to His people, the Jews. From their own Scriptures they should have recognized Him immediately as the Son of God. But we are told, "... The Jews require a sign." (See 1 Corinthians 1:22; John 4:48.) A "miracle" is a *sign*. Only a few days before, John the Baptist had heralded Jesus as the One sent by God. This first miracle (sign) was one of many to prove to the Jews that Jesus is indeed God the Son.

3. Why would the Spirit of God carefully record for us that this was the *first* miracle of the Lord Jesus? (See John 1:11.) It was to show His glory. (John 2:11b). In the chapter before the record of this first miracle, we read, "And the Word was made flesh, and dwelt among us (and we beheld His glory, the glory as of the only begotten of the Father), full of grace and truth" (John 1:14).

   Before the coming of the Lord Jesus, the Jews knew that God was among them by seeing in their place of worship a great cloud of light. It was known as the *Shekinah glory*. When the Lord Jesus came to earth, He, the light of the world, was the glory of God.

4. Our Lord spoke of "His hour" when He spoke to Mary. What did He mean by "His hour"? In the Gospels we see this expression repeatedly. (See John 7:30; 8:20; 13:1; 17:1; Matthew 26:45.) Mary knew what others at the feast did not know. She had known, even before the Lord Jesus had come to earth, that He was the Son of God. (See Luke 1:35.) Before His coming, she had spoken of her Saviour (Luke 1:47). At His birth, when the shepherds came to worship Him "Mary kept all these things and pondered them in her heart" (Luke 2:19). When He was a child, He was in the house of God astonishing the doctors. And "His mother kept all these sayings in her heart" (Luke 2:51).

   For more than 30 years she had known Him to be the Son of God. Now she probably wanted Him to let others know this. That He was God the Son could never be fully understood, He knew, until He died on the cross. That was "His hour." And He told His mother that day that the hour for which He had come into the world (for He had come to die), had not yet come.

5. The waterpots at the feast were there, we are told, "after the manner of the purifying of the Jews." The Jews had many ceremonial rites. (See, for example, Mark 7:3,4. Also: Leviticus 12:2-4; Numbers 19:1-10.) A thoughtful, religious host, would have water for his guests to wash themselves before eating.

Scripture to be studied: John 2:1-11

The *aim* of the lesson: To show that the Saviour has all power.

   What your students should *know*: (1) The Lord Jesus is the Creator (John 1:3; Colossians 1:16-17). (2) The Lord Jesus has all power (Hebrews 1:3). (3) The all powerful Creator, the Lord Jesus, is the Saviour of the world.

   What your students should *feel*: A desire to have Jesus change their lives.

   What your students should *do*: Believe that Jesus is the Son of God who paid the punishment for sin; receive Him as Saviour.

Lesson outline (for the teacher's and students' notebooks):

1. A need at the wedding (John 2:1-3).
2. The need brought to Jesus (John 2:3-5).
3. Jesus meets the need (John 2:6-8).
4. Power to give the best (John 2:9-11).

The verse to be memorized:

The Father sent the Son to be the Saviour of the world. (1 John 4:14)

NOTE TO THE TEACHER

These men who saw the Son of God with their very own eyes knew at once that He was truly the Lamb of God.

If you are walking daily with Him, reading His Word, talking with Him in prayer, His presence is real to you. Then you will be able to make Him known to your pupils. May it be said of you: "These are they which follow the Lamb whithersoever He goeth" (Revelation 14:4b).

THE LESSON
1. A NEED AT THE WEDDING
John 2:1-3

It was a happy day in the little town of Cana in Galilee. There was a wedding to which many had come. Mary, the mother of Jesus, came from nearby Nazareth. But the most important of all guests was there–Jesus Christ. His newly chosen disciples, Andrew, John, Peter, Philip and Nathanael, had also come.

Most of the guests at the wedding feast did not think of the Lord Jesus as being different from anyone else. They did not recognize Him as the Lamb of God, the Saviour of the world. Many may never have seen Him. His disciples did not yet know very much about Him. They had been with Him only a few days.

At the feast everything was going well. The man in charge must have been pleased to see the happiness of the guests.

Show Illustration #5

Suddenly something went wrong. There was no more wine! Not a drop! Perhaps more guests had come than had been expected. The servants didn't want the man in charge of the feast to know that the wine was gone. They didn't want the bride and bridegroom to know. What were they going to do?

2. THE NEED BROUGHT TO JESUS
John 2:3-5

When Mary, the mother of Jesus, learned of the problem she immediately thought of Jesus. He could help the servants, surely. He always knew the right thing to do. Perhaps she hoped that He would at this time do something to prove to all the people that He was the Son of God. Mary knew who Jesus really was. She wanted everyone else to know.

Show Illustration #6

She hurried to the Lord Jesus. "They have no wine," she told Him.

"What is it you want Me to do?" Jesus asked her. Because He knew what was in her heart, He told her His secret: "My hour is not yet come."

Not until He would die could they *fully* understand that He is God the Son. And it was not yet time for Him to die.

Only this once, in all the Word of God, do we read of people going to Mary. When they did, she sent them to Jesus!

Mary turned to the servants saying, "Whatever He tells you to do, do it."

3. JESUS MEETS THE NEED
John 2:6-8

Immediately the servants went to the Lord Jesus. He commanded, "Fill the waterpots with water."

Show Illustration #7

They obeyed Him at once, filling the waterpots right to the brim. They probably thought as they filled 1, 2, 3, 4, 5, 6 waterpots: *What will He ever do with all this water? It is wine we need. Not water!*

When the waterpots were filled, the Lord Jesus said, "Now give a drink to the master of the feast."

The servants doubtless wondered what would happen when they took plain water to the man in charge of the feast. He wanted wine! No matter what the servants thought, they obeyed. They poured what they thought was water into a cup. But it did not look like water. It was not water. It was wine–good, pure wine!

4. POWER TO GIVE THE BEST
John 2:9-11

The Lord Jesus had done a miracle! He had turned water into wine. But He had been turning water into wine from the beginning of time. "All things were made by Him; and without Him was not any thing made that was made," we are told. (See John 1:3.) The uncounted thousands of vines covering the hillsides–all were made by Him. The grapes that grew on those vines were grapes of His making. Usually it took many months for vines and grapes to grow. This time He, the Creator, had chosen to make the wine in a moment. He who has all power can do anything!

Show Illustration #8

When the servants took the wine to the man in charge of the feast, he tasted it. He must have thought, *This is the best wine I have ever had!* He went to the bridegroom and said, "Usually a man serves good wine first. Then, when everyone has had plenty to drink, he brings out the poor wine. But you have kept the best wine until last."

The bridegroom was as puzzled as the man in charge of the feast. He could not explain what had happened for he did not know!

That was a wonderful day for the newly chosen disciples. They had believed that Jesus was the Lamb of God, the Saviour of the world. Now they knew that He is God the Son, the Creator, the all-powerful One. With their own eyes they had seen His glory. They were happy to be His disciples, His pupils, His followers.

It is wonderful that the Lord Jesus changed water to wine in an instant. But He has power to do something far more wonderful: He can change your life. He waits right now to cleanse your heart from sin and fill it with His love and joy. He can do it in an instant.

Do you believe that Jesus is God the Son? Do you believe that He took your punishment for sin? Will you ask Him to forgive you? How is it that He has the right to forgive sin? Because He is the Saviour. Will you receive Him as *your* Saviour? Will you do it right now? The moment you do this, He will make you a "new creature." (See 2 Corinthians 5:17.)

NOTE TO THE TEACHER

Before you teach the next lesson, spend time alone with God. Ask Him to help you to make these truths clear:

1. The Lord Jesus is the Creator (John 1:3; Colossians 1:16, 17).
2. The Lord Jesus has all power (Hebrews 1:3).
3. The all-powerful Creator, the Lord Jesus, is the Saviour of the world.

It is a glorious thing to know that He, by whom all things came into existence, came into this world to suffer for our sins for one purpose: that we might have everlasting life.

Lesson 3
NICODEMUS AND THE NEW BIRTH

Scripture to be studied: John 3:1-21

The *aim* of the lesson: To show that Jesus Christ is the One who gives eternal life.

What your students should *know*: To live in Heaven forever, one must be born again.

What your students should *feel*: A desire to be born again.

What your students should *do*: Receive the Lord Jesus Christ as Saviour.

Lesson outline (for the teacher's and students' notebooks):
1. Religious leaders listen to Jesus (John 2:23).
2. Nicodemus learns about the new birth (John 3:1-10).
3. Nicodemus learns the need for faith (John 3:11-13).
4. Eternal life for those who believe in Christ (John 3:14-21).

The verse to be memorized:

The Father sent the Son to be the Saviour of the world. (1 John 4:14)

NOTE TO THE TEACHER

In Lesson #1, the Lord Jesus is presented as the Lamb of God. In Lesson #2, He is proved to be the all-powerful Saviour. In this lesson you have the privilege of presenting Christ as the One who gives life–new life–eternal life!

Ask God to help you, through teaching about Nicodemus, to present the new birth so that each listener will sense the importance of being born into the family of God. The need to be born again is the same for everyone: rich or poor, young or old, big or little, good or bad. Nicodemus was a good man, well educated, important. But he needed to be born again!

THE LESSON

There are many kinds of families in this world. There are cat families. There are families of dogs. Pigs have families. There are chicken families. There are families of people. Did you ever hear of a cat being born into a dog family? Or have you known of pigs being born into chicken families? Of course not. Pigs are in families of pigs. Dogs are in families of dogs. And people are in families of people.

God has made everything this way. He tells us in His Word, however, that people born once into earthly families can also be born into His family. That may seem impossible. But with God nothing is impossible! Not only is it possible to become a child of God by being born into the family of God, we learn today that unless a person *is* born into the family of God, we can never, never, never go to be with God in His Heaven-home. Listen carefully to what the Lord Jesus taught.

1. RELIGIOUS LEADERS LISTEN TO JESUS
John 2:23

In the city of Jerusalem crowds of people saw the Lord Jesus do great miracles. Because of His miracles, many people believed in Him. (See John 2:23.)

Show Illustration #9

Among those who listened to Jesus and watched Him do His miracles were the Pharisees. The Pharisees were religious leaders who were very strict about obeying the laws which God had given. They also made up many laws of their own. The Pharisees believed that living by strict rules, they were better than anyone–even better than the Lord Jesus! They were proud of their laws. When they listened to the Lord Jesus talk, they tried to show their own importance. Often they spoke right out and said unkind things about the Son of God. They were jealous of Him and did not want others to believe in Him.

2. NICODEMUS LEARNS ABOUT THE NEW BIRTH
John 3:1-10

There was one Pharisee, however, who was different from the rest. His name was Nicodemus. Although he was an important ruler and teacher of the Jews, he did not speak out against Jesus. Instead he listened carefully to what Jesus said. As Nicodemus listened, he decided to find out more about this Person who could do such great miracles. But how would it be possible to learn more about the Lord Jesus? He could not talk to Him when the crowds were around. Nor could he talk to Jesus when the other Pharisees were there. They would be angry with him, perhaps even laugh at him.

Show Illustration #10

Nicodemus made up his mind what he would do. One night, when no one could see him, Nicodemus went to the home where Jesus was staying. Away from the crowds and away from his Pharisee friends, Nicodemus looked into the face of the Son of God. The Lord Jesus, Nicodemus knew, was no ordinary man. His miracles were proof enough to Nicodemus that Jesus was Someone special.

"Master," Nicodemus said, "we know that You are a teacher come from God. No man could do the mighty works You do unless God were with Him."

The Lord Jesus did not thank Nicodemus for his nice words. Instead, He looked into the mind and heart of Nicodemus. He knew all about this man and his questions. So He went at once to the point. Jesus said, "Except a man is born again, he cannot see the Kingdom of God."

What a strange thing for Jesus to say! Nicodemus did not understand. Did Jesus mean that he, Nicodemus the Pharisee, could not get to Heaven? He had been careful to obey all the laws and rules of the Pharisees. He was a good-living man. But now the Lord Jesus had said that *no one* could see the Kingdom of God without being born again.

Nicodemus asked, "How can a man be born when he is old?"

The Lord Jesus then told Nicodemus that the second birth is different from the first birth. The first birth has to do with the body and the way we look on the outside. That first birth is necessary if one is to live on earth. But the second birth has to do with the spirit–the way we are in our hearts. The second birth is not seen. Just as we cannot see the wind or know where it comes from or where it goes, so we cannot see the second birth because it is a spiritual one. That second birth is necessary if one is to live in Heaven.

Poor Nicodemus! It was all new to him. He could not understand what the Lord Jesus meant. He had never before heard of a spiritual birth.

"How can it be?" he asked.

"Nicodemus," the Lord Jesus asked, "are you a teacher of the Jews and do not know these things?"

3. NICODEMUS LEARNS THE NEED FOR FAITH
John 3:11-13

Show Illustration #11

Jesus reminded Nicodemus of something that had occurred many hundreds of years before. It had happened to the people of God (the Israelites) when they were traveling across the wilderness from Egypt to the land which God had promised them. (See Numbers 21:5-9.) In the wilderness the people spoke against God. And God punished them for their sin by sending snakes to bite them. Many men and women and boys and girls had died. The people cried to God for help. So God had told their leader (Moses) to make a snake out of shining brass and put it on the top of a high pole. When the people who had been bitten looked at the brass serpent, they were made well. But if they did not look at the brass serpent, they died.

4. ETERNAL LIFE FOR THOSE WHO BELIEVE IN CHRIST
John 3:14-21

Show Illustration #12

So Jesus said to Nicodemus, "As Moses lifted up the serpent in the wilderness, even so must the Son of Man be lifted up. Anyone who believes in Him will not perish, but will have everlasting life."

This means that as the people of God had to use faith and look at the serpent of brass to prevent physical death, to prevent eternal death, we must look to Jesus, the Lamb of God, who died on the cross for us.

What good news this was to Nicodemus! At last he understood how to get into the family of God. He had to be born into it. How was he to be born again? Not by keeping the Law as did the Pharisees, but by believing on the Lord Jesus as his own Saviour. There is no other way to get to Heaven.

Nicodemus couldn't forget the things Jesus had told him. Jesus had revealed to him that He, the Son of God, was going to die on a cross. (See John 3:14.) He had explained that the person who didn't believe in Him was already condemned to eternal death (being forever separated from God and all that is good and pure and holy). But God wants everyone in the world to be saved. That is why He allowed His Son to take the punishment of sin for everyone. To believe in Him means that the believer is *not* condemned. Instead he has life–everlasting life. He will spend forever with God and the Lord Jesus in Heaven.

While the Bible does not say that Nicodemus was born again, we believe he did become a child of God either that night or later. (See John 7:50; 19:39.)

Is it perfectly clear to you what is meant by the *new birth*? Try to think of things that happened when you were born the first time. What is the very first thing you received when you were born into your earthly family?

NOTE TO THE TEACHER

Print these words on separate sheets of paper. Then fold them so that as you unfold the paper, each new word appears.

LIFE	HOME	RIGHTEOUS-
WASHED	EVERLAST-	NESS
CLOTHED	ING LIFE	GOD
FATHER	BLOOD	CHRISTIAN
NAME		HEAVEN

LIFE . . . The moment you came into this world, someone probably spanked you a little. You took a big breath and cried loudly. You had life!

Next, you were

WASHED . . . Someone took that tiny baby, you, and washed you clean.

Then you were

CLOTHED . . . Your parents had probably prepared for your coming by having some nice clothes ready.

You had a mother, of course. But you had, also, a

FATHER . . . Oh, he was proud of you! Then your parents talked it over and decided upon a

NAME . . . That is the name that you are known by even today.

Another thing you received the first time you were born: a

HOME . . . All of these things were yours when you were born the first time. To be born into your earthly family is good. You wouldn't be living on earth if you had not been born once.

But if you are ever to live with God in His Heaven–you must be born into His family. Exactly what happens when one is born into the family of God? First, that person gets *life*–

EVERLASTING LIFE . . . As you received the kind of life your parents had by being born the first time, you receive the kind of life God has, when you are born into His family. As God is everlasting, so the kind of life He gives is everlasting.

Being born into the family of God means you must he washed. But washing with water will not cleanse your sins. Your heart must be *cleansed* by the precious

BLOOD . . . The blood of the Lord Jesus Christ. When He died on the cross He took upon Himself your sin. (See Isaiah 53:6; 1 Peter 2:24.) When you believe that He is the Son of God and receive Him as your sin-bearer, He cleanses your heart by His precious blood. Your heart is made clean. You may not *understand* how it can be. But you must *believe* that it is so. (See John 3:15, 16, 18.)

When you are born into the family of God, you get *clothes* . . .

RIGHTEOUSNESS clothes, the Bible tells us. (See Isaiah 61:10.) This means you are in right standing with God the moment you truly believe in the Lord Jesus, the Son of God.

To be born into the family of God means you have a new

FATHER . . . God. You become His child when you receive His Son as Saviour.

You get a new *name* when you are a member of God's family:

CHRISTIAN . . . *One belonging to Christ*, is what your new name means.

And you get a new *home*. It is

HEAVEN . . . To have the Lord Jesus in your heart and life is to be assured that one day you will be forever with Him.

To live on earth, you must be born once. If you are to live in Heaven forever, you must be born again. Who makes it possible for you to be born again? The Saviour, the Lord Jesus Christ.

Have *you* been born again? If not, will you receive the Lord Jesus Christ as your Saviour right now?

Lesson 4
THE SAVIOUR

The *aim* of the lesson: To show that there is only one Saviour. Therefore, there is only one way to be saved.

What your students should *know*: Everyone needs a Saviour from sin, because all have sinned and come short of the goodness of God.

What your students should *feel*: Conscious of their sin and need for a Saviour.

What your students should *do*:
  Unsaved: Receive the Lord Jesus as Saviour.
  Saved: Tell others that Jesus died for their sins,

Lesson outline (for the teacher's and students' notebooks):
1. The whole world needs the Saviour (Romans 3:23).
2. Jesus saves from the penalty of sin (Ephesians 2:8-9).
3. Jesus saves from the power of sin (1 John 1:9).
4. Jesus saves from the presence of sin (1 John 3:1-3).

The verse to be memorized:

The Father sent the Son to be the Saviour of the world. (1 John 4:14)

> **NOTE TO THE TEACHER**
>
> Do you count it a privilege to teach the doctrines of God's Word? When studying and teaching the doctrine of *The Saviour*, your heart will be filled with praise for such a great salvation.
>
> There are three main thoughts which your students should write (and, if possible, illustrate) in their notebooks:
> 1. Christ alone can set a person free from the *penalty* of sin.
> 2. Christ alone can free a person from the *power* of sin.
> 3. Christ alone will, in the future, set His own free from the *presence* of sin.

By now we have this verse learned by memory. Is it stored away in your heart?

Everyone has a name. It may be Mary, Becky, Michael, Juan, or Isaac. (*Teacher:* Use the names of pupils in your class.) Whatever your name, it is important. Some names have special meanings. (*Teacher:* If possible, you could give the meanings of some of the names of those in your class.)

There is one name that is more wonderful and more important than any other name. That name is *Jesus*. His name was not chosen by Mary, His mother. It was given by God. Before Jesus came to earth, God sent an angel to Mary with this good news: "You are to have a Son, and you are to name Him Jesus" (Luke 1:31).

Mary was happy with the name God had chosen for the Child. She said, "I rejoice in God my Saviour" (Luke 1:47). Of whom was she speaking when she said this? She was speaking about Jesus. Why did Mary say, "God *my Saviour*"? She was saying that she, like everyone else, needed a Saviour–*One who could save her from her sin.*

Joseph (who was later to become the husband of Mary) also had good news from an angel. It was this: "Mary will have a Son. You are to call His name JESUS: for *He shall save His people from their sins*" (Matthew 1:21).

When the Lord Jesus came to earth, the angel announced it to the shepherds this way: "Unto you is born this day . . . a *Saviour, which is Christ the Lord*" (Luke 2:11).

Each time we say the words of our memory verse, we should remember what the angel told Mary, Joseph and the shepherds: Jesus Christ the Lord is *the Saviour, the Saviour of the world.*

Think of the verse this way: "God the Father sent His Son to be the Saviour of the world." Never, never forget that this was the reason that the Son of God left His wonderful home in Heaven: to be the *Saviour* of the world.

THE LESSON

Often in this class and in your study of God's Book, you hear and see these words: *Saviour; salvation; saved.* These words should be in your notebook, along with the meaning of each.

1. THE WHOLE WORLD NEEDS THE SAVIOUR
Romans 3:23

All of those who heard the announcement of the angels regarding the coming of the Son of God to earth, understood that He was (and is!) the Saviour. What does the word saviour mean? A person who saves another person from drowning, for example, could be said to be a saviour. The drowning person is made safe–he is saved–by the Saviour. When God the Father sent His Son to earth, He sent Him to save us from something far worse than drowning. He sent Him to save us from sin. When we believe that the Lord Jesus is the Son of God; when we believe that He, the *Saviour,* died for our sins to make us safe from the penalty of sin, we are saved–saved from eternal separation from God. (In our next series we will learn more about this.) When we are *saved* by the *Saviour,* we have *salvation.*

(*Teacher:* Take time to have your students write the preceding truths in their notebooks. Throughout the balance of the lesson, use as many questions as possible to help your students think and to tell what they know!)

How many people need a Saviour from sin? (*The answer: Everyone needs the Saviour.*)

Why does everyone need a Saviour? (*Because* all *have sinned and come short of the perfect goodness of God.*)

Show Illustration #13

Let us suppose for a moment that right next to us is a deep river with a strong current. Maybe you are a good swimmer and have swum from one side of the river to the other many times. But today as you swim, the current is stronger than ever. You swim with all your strength. But the water is too strong for you. You lose your breath. The current pulls you away and down under the water, beating you fiercely against the rocks. Suppose, as you come to the surface gasping for breath, you would cry, "I'm a good person! I don't lie! I don't steal! I've done many good things for others!" Would the good things you have done save you from drowning?

– 24 –

When you came up the second time from the depths of the river, suppose you cried, "My parents are good people! They always go church! I have gone to church! I gave money to the church!" Would having good parents or going to church save you from drowning?

No! What you need is someone who can rescue you–one who is a better swimmer than you; one who is stronger than the raging river. That person becomes your saviour from drowning.

2. JESUS SAVES FROM THE PENALTY OF SIN
Ephesians 2:8-9

Show Illustration #14

God knew that the sin in this world would pull you down and away from Him into eternal death. Jesus Christ the Lord is the Son of God. He is absolutely perfect and without sin. He is the Saviour. What did He do that causes us know that He is the Saviour? He died on the cross, *taking the penalty [punishment] for your sin*. He is (as we learned in Lesson #1) the Lamb of God who takes away the sin of the world. How do we know that He is the Saviour sent from God? He rose again from the dead. He had victory over death. And He lives today in Heaven, the home of God.

Once we receive Him as Saviour from the *penalty of sin*, do we still need a Saviour? Indeed we do! Our past sins are forgiven when we receive the Lord Jesus as Saviour. However, because we have the same bodies, we may still do wrong things. The wrongs after salvation may be quite different from the wrongs we did before we were saved. We may be unkind to another. Or we may tell something that is not the whole truth. Or maybe we do not work as hard as we should. Any of these things is like a weight, holding us back from being all that we should be. (See Hebrews 12:1.)

3. JESUS SAVES FROM THE POWER OF SIN
(1 John 1:9)

Show Illustration #15

In a race we could run with a light weight tied to our back. Add more weights and it becomes harder to run. It is possible to have so many weights tied to one's back, that the runner can no longer run. His weights have power over him. If he is to win the race, there must be no weights.

So it is when we are saved. The sins–even small ones–are weights. And the Saviour can save His child from *the power of sin*. He does this if we confess our sins to Him. That is, we must tell Him (even though He already knows) exactly what wrong thing we have done. We must purpose that with His help we will never do that wrong thing again. It is then that He forgives our sin. (See 1 John 1:9.)

How do we know that the Saviour has such power? He proved it by the miracles that He did. Turning water into wine in a moment of time, for example, proved His great power.

What is the Saviour doing now, this moment? He is praying for you. (See Hebrews 7:24-27.) He prays that you will not be discouraged even when the way is hard. He prays that you will find the way of escape whenever you are tempted to sin. (See 1 Corinthians 10:13.)

4. JESUS SAVES FROM THE PRESENCE OF SIN
1 John 3:1-3

It is a wonderful thing to be saved from *the penalty of sin* and from *the power of sin*. But here is one more wonderful truth: some day, when we are in Heaven with the Saviour, Jesus, we will be saved from *the presence of sin*. That is, we will never see, or hear, or do, a wrong thing. We will be like the Lord Jesus Himself.

Show Illustration #16

Suppose we had here a type of worm, surrounded by fire. Whichever direction the worm turns, he meets fire. There is no escape. However, if you would reach down into the center of the flame he could climb up your finger–or you could pick him up and remove him from the fire. You remove him from the circle of fire and he is saved from its presence.

Today, we who are believers in the Lord Jesus Christ are surrounded by sin. We see sinful things; we hear things that are sinful; we think sinful thoughts. We hate sin–all of it.

But a day is coming when those who have been saved by the Saviour, will be taken by Him to His Heaven-home. We shall be removed from the presence of sin. Do you think that will be a happy day? Indeed it will! And what do you suppose we will say when we are taken from *the presence of sin*? This: "Worthy is the Lamb that was slain" (Revelation 5:12). Always we will praise the One who "loved us, and washed us from our sins in His own blood" (Revelation 1:5).

How long will we be away from the presence of sin? Forever and forever and forever. When we are saved, as Nicodemus was told in Lesson #3, we receive eternal life–life that is forever.

If you are saved, you can say:
God loves *me*.
I have sinned.
Jesus, the Saviour, died for *me*.
I have received the Lord Jesus as *my* Saviour.
Now *I* have everlasting life.

And you can say to others:
God loves *you*.
You have sinned.
The Saviour, Jesus, died for *you*.
If you will receive Him as *your* Saviour,
You will have everlasting life.

Remember that having *everlasting life* means:
1. We are saved from *the penalty of sin* (the penalty of being forever separated from God).
2. We are saved from *the power of sin* (the sins we may do after we are saved).
3. We shall be saved from *the presence of sin* (when we are in Heaven with the Saviour).

www.ingramcontent.com/pod-product-compliance
Lightning Source LLC
Chambersburg PA
CBHW060807090426
42736CB00002B/193